3065

Bennett School
820 Bennett St
Jackson, MI 49202

"There is no problem that we can't solve if we can corral our resources behind it. That means people, that means money, that means the good will and cooperation of a large segment of the people."

— CORETTA SCOTT KING

CORETTA SCOTT KING

BY CYNTHIA KLINGEL

GRAPHIC DESIGN
Robert E. Bonaker / Graphic Design & Consulting Co.

PROJECT COORDINATOR
James R. Rothaus / James R. Rothaus & Associates

EDITORIAL DIRECTION
Elizabeth Sirimarco

PHOTO RESEARCH
Ann Schwab / The Child's World, Inc.

COVER PHOTO
Portrait of Coretta Scott King / UPI/Corbis-Bettmann

Library of Congress Cataloging-in-Publication Data
Klingel, Cynthia Fitterer
Coretta Scott King / by Cynthia Klingel
p. cm.
Summary: A brief biography of the wife of the Reverend Martin
Luther King, Jr., who shared his dedication to working peaceably
to achieve equality for all Americans.
ISBN 1-56766-567-5 (library reinforced : alk. paper)

1. King, Coretta Scott, 1927-   — Juvenile literature. 2. Afro-
American women — Biography — Juvenile literature. 3. Afro-
Americans — Biography — Juvenile literature. 4. Civil rights
workers — United States — Biography — Juvenile literature.
5. Civil rights movement — United States — History — 20th
century — Juvenile literature. 6. King, Martin Luther, Jr. 1929-
1968 — Juvenile literature.
[1. King, Coretta Scott, 1927-   . 2. Civil rights workers. 3. Afro-
Americans — Biography. 4. Women — Biography. 5. King, Martin
Luther, Jr., 1929-1968.] I. Title

E185.97.K47K57 1999   98-27012
323'.092— dc21   CIP
[B]   AC

Contents

Growing Up in Alabama

When Coretta Scott was a young girl, she lived with her family in a tiny home with just two rooms, a kitchen and a bedroom. It was a small place for five people to live. The floors were bare wood, and the paper peeled off the walls. The family carried water from a well in the backyard. It wasn't very different from the way other *African Americans* lived in Alabama at the time, but Coretta's father, Obadiah (or Obie) Scott, wanted more for his family.

Coretta was born on April 27, 1927, two years before the *Great Depression* of 1929. During the Depression, thousands of Americans lost their jobs, and many people barely had enough to eat. Although the Scotts didn't have much money, they did have a small farm where they could raise animals and grow vegetables. The whole family chipped in to make sure they always had food on the table.

Coretta's older sister was named Edythe. They had a younger brother, Obie, who was named after their father. All three of the Scott children woke up at dawn to feed the chickens and hogs. They also found time to milk the cows before it was time to go to school. In the summer, they helped their mother tend a large vegetable garden. The children also worked for neighbors, chopping wood and picking cotton to help pay for school.

Mr. Scott worked the hardest of all. In addition to running the family farm, he worked long hours at a lumber mill and even opened a small barber shop in their home. Once he saved enough money to buy a truck, Mr. Scott began hauling lumber for the mill operator at night and on weekends.

A FARM WORKER AND HIS CHILDREN ARRIVE HOME AFTER A LONG DAY WORKING IN TOBACCO FIELDS. DURING THE FIRST HALF OF THE 20TH CENTURY, AFRICAN AMERICANS IN THE SOUTH LABORED AT ANY JOB THEY COULD FIND TO SUPPORT THEIR FAMILIES. OBIE SCOTT WANTED THE BEST FOR HIS FAMILY, AND THAT MEANT A LOT OF HARD WORK.

Ed Eckstein/Corbis

MEMBERS OF THE KU KLUX KLAN, A RACIST ORGANIZATION THAT BELIEVES WHITES ARE SUPERIOR TO ALL OTHER RACES, HAVE OFTEN BEEN ACCUSED OF SETTING FIRE TO THE PROPERTY OF AFRICAN AMERICANS. PREJUDICE WAS A DIFFICULT FACT OF LIFE FOR THE SCOTTS, WHO LOST THEIR HOME WHEN IT WAS BURNED TO THE GROUND, PROBABLY BY WHITE SOUTHERNERS WHO HAD THREATENED OBIE.

No matter how hard the Scotts worked, things were not easy for them — or for other African Americans who lived in the South during the 1930s. Mr. Scott was the only African American in the county who owned a truck. White truck owners were afraid he would take business away from them, and they often threatened him.

After a lot of effort, Mr. Scott finally saved enough money to buy his own mill. When a White man tried to buy it from him, he refused, and only a few days later, the mill was burned to the ground. Mr. Scott knew that by trying to build a better life for his family, he had put himself in danger.

Because of Obie's dedication, his family was able to move into a much bigger home when Coretta was 10 years old. The six rooms felt like a palace. There was a living room with fine, new furniture, and Coretta and Edythe had their own bedroom.

Only five years later, it was all gone. On Thanksgiving Day in 1942, the family's beautiful home burned down. The Scotts felt certain that the White men who had been threatening Obie for so long were responsible, but they believed it would do no good to ask the sheriff to investigate. It seemed as if no one cared what happened to Black Americans in the South.

The house fire was the most difficult lesson about *prejudice* the Scott family learned, but it certainly wasn't the first.

A LABORER AT A SOUTHERN MILL BUNDLES LARGE PLANKS OF LUMBER.

USDA Forest Service/Corbis

Struggling for an Education

When Coretta was growing up in the South, Whites and Blacks were *segregated*, or kept apart, from each other. Black children couldn't go to school with White children, or even drink from the same water fountain. At the movies, Coretta and her friends had to sit in the hot, crowded balcony. White children could sit in comfortable seats on the main floor.

Coretta, Edythe, and young Obie went to the Crossroads School in Heiberger, a school for African American children in the area. Every day, rain or shine, they walked three miles to school, and three miles home again. Every day, the school bus rumbled past, carrying White children to their own school.

Coretta knew the White children had a fine brick school with separate rooms for each grade and a library filled with books. At the Crossroads School, more than 100 children were crowded into a single, shabby room. Two teachers struggled to teach six grades, and there were never enough books for all of the students.

With these problems, it wasn't easy for the children at Coretta's school to complete all six grades, and it was almost impossible for them to go on to attend high school. The closest high school for African American students was 20 miles from the Scott's home. There were no school buses for Blacks, although White students were bused to Marion High School, which was only 10 miles away.

Coretta's mother had only a fourth-grade education herself, but she was determined her children would go to high school. She arranged for Coretta and Edythe to stay with a family in Marion where they could attend a private high school for African Americans called Lincoln School.

SCHOOLS IN THE SOUTH WERE STILL SEGREGATED WHEN CORETTA WAS A GIRL. AFRICAN AMERICANS COULD NOT ATTEND THE SAME SCHOOLS AS WHITE CHILDREN.

At first, the Scott girls were the only Black children from their community fortunate enough to attend high school. Most families couldn't afford to pay for their children's room and board in faraway Marion. Then, when Coretta was a junior in high school, her father converted one of his trucks into a makeshift bus. Although it meant a 40-mile trip each day, Mrs. Scott drove all the African American children from their area to and from school. Not only could more children attend Lincoln School, Coretta could return home to live with her family.

Lincoln School opened a whole new world to Coretta. It was as good as the White high schools in the area. The teachers, some of whom were White, believed Black children deserved as good an education as White children. Some people in Marion threatened the White teachers and called them names for choosing to teach and work with African Americans.

Coretta earned top grades in all her subjects, but she enjoyed music most of all. Her teachers complimented her beautiful voice. She took voice lessons, sang in the choir, and learned to play both the trumpet and the piano.

During her senior year, Coretta learned she had won a *scholarship* to Antioch College in Yellow Springs, Ohio. Edythe was already a student at Antioch, and Coretta was happy to join her. She was also ready to leave the South. Coretta knew that African Americans struggled less against *racism* and prejudice in the northern states.

The years at Antioch went quickly as Coretta continued to study music. She was one of only six Black students, but Coretta made friends with all her classmates. She had planned to become a teacher, but during her last year at Antioch, her teachers urged her to continue studying music. They thought she was talented enough to become a concert singer. Before graduating, she applied for a grant to study at the New England Conservatory of Music in Boston.

AP Wide World Photos

CORETTA HAD A BEAUTIFUL SINGING VOICE, AND SHE STUDIED MUSIC IN COLLEGE. SHE WOULD USE HER TALENT MANY YEARS LATER, PERFORMING AT CONCERTS GIVEN IN THE NAME OF PEACE AND FREEDOM.

Coretta Meets Martin Luther King, Jr.

Coretta won a small scholarship to attend the New England Conservatory of Music, but she still needed to earn money to help pay for school. She kept a busy schedule, studying, attending classes, and working at small jobs, until she received financial aid from the state of Alabama. Coretta was able to stop working so much and devote more time to her studies. Ironically, the money was given only to African American college students who studied at schools outside the state. Those who chose to study at Alabama colleges were not eligible for the state's financial aid. The system seemed to encourage Blacks to leave the state.

In Boston, Coretta's studies kept her so busy, she didn't have many opportunities to meet people, and sometimes she was lonely. One day, a friend told her about a young man from Atlanta named Martin Luther King, Jr., a minister who was studying at Boston University. Martin wanted to meet her.

Coretta agreed to have lunch with him. They liked each other, and soon they were spending as much time together as their studies would allow. Martin often mentioned marriage, but Coretta was not interested at first. She wanted to pursue a career as an opera singer, and it was clear that he wanted a wife who would put their marriage and family first.

Gene Herrick/AP Wide World

CORETTA AND MARTIN LUTHER KING, JR., WERE DEDICATED
TO ONE ANOTHER ALMOST FROM THE MOMENT THEY MET.

Globe Photos

CORETTA RESPECTED MARTIN'S BELIEFS AND
RECOGNIZED THAT HE WAS A GIFTED SPEAKER
WHO COULD MAKE PEOPLE THINK.

The more Martin talked about his goals in life, the more Coretta realized they were the same as hers. Like Coretta, he wanted to help African Americans get a good education and decent jobs. He wanted to help Blacks achieve *civil rights*. Coretta decided to marry Martin, even though it meant she would not have a singing career. In 1953, less than a year after they met, Coretta and Martin were married in a ceremony at her family's home. After the wedding, the couple returned to Boston to complete their studies.

Once he finished school, Martin had many job offers, many of them in the North. After living in Boston, the newlyweds knew it would be difficult to return to the segregated South, but they decided it was their duty to return. It was in the South where their efforts could make the most difference. In 1954, Martin accepted a position at the Dexter Avenue Baptist Church in Montgomery, Alabama.

CORETTA AND MARTIN MOVED BACK TO ALABAMA WHEN HE ACCEPTED A JOB AT THE DEXTER AVENUE BAPTIST CHURCH.

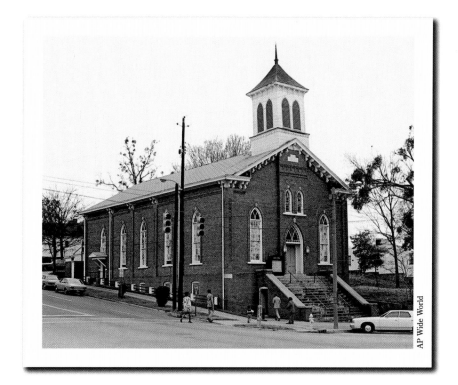

AP Wide World

Back in the South

Coretta had nearly forgotten what life was like for Black people in the South. In Alabama, she and Martin had to use elevators, drinking fountains, and restrooms marked "colored," a term used at the time to describe African Americans. They had to eat in "colored" restaurants. They couldn't even enter public buildings through the same door as White people.

The Montgomery Bus Company had its own set of unjust rules. The seats in the front of the buses were for Whites only. Black people had to sit in the rear. If all the front seats in the bus were taken, Blacks had to give up their seats to Whites. Blacks even had to pay their fares at the front of the bus, get off, and then board again through the rear door. Sometimes a driver would pull away without a Black passenger after he or she had paid the fare.

On December 1, 1955, a woman named Rosa Parks refused to give up her seat to a White man. The police arrested Ms. Parks and took her to jail. The African American citizens of Montgomery decided they had had enough. Martin wondered what would happen if Blacks stopped riding the bus in protest, and he suggested the idea of a bus *boycott*. A message was passed among the city's 50,000 African Americans telling them not to ride the bus to work, to town, to school, or anywhere else on Monday, December 5.

UPI/Corbis-Bettmann

ROSA PARKS RIDES IN THE FRONT OF A MONTGOMERY BUS AFTER THE
BUS BOYCOTT CAME TO AN END IN DECEMBER 1956, ONE YEAR AFTER
SHE REFUSED TO GIVE UP HER SEAT TO A WHITE MAN.

THE KINGS QUICKLY BECAME WELL KNOWN
IN MONTGOMERY AFTER MARTIN ORGANIZED
THE BUS BOYCOTT.

On the day of the boycott, Martin and Coretta King were up at 5:30 in the morning. The first bus was due to drive past their house in just half an hour. As its headlights pierced the darkness, Coretta stood at the window, straining to see inside. There was not a single person on the usually crowded bus. Almost no one rode the bus that day. Some people went to work in cars, others on foot. Some took taxis or rode bicycles, and some even arrived at their destinations in horse-drawn buggies.

That afternoon, many of the community's Black leaders met to create a list of their demands. They did not ask that African Americans be permitted to sit anywhere they wanted on Montgomery buses. Instead, they asked only that bus drivers treat them politely and that Black people not be forced to give up their seats to Whites. The group resolved to encourage the community to boycott the Montgomery Bus Company until these goals were reached.

AP Wide World Photos

AN EMPTY MONTGOMERY BUS CONTINUES ON ITS ROUTE IN APRIL 1956. THE BUS BOYCOTT WENT ON FOR MORE THAN A YEAR.

Martin organized a meeting that evening, and 5,000 African Americans attended. They agreed to continue the boycott until the demands were met. Black citizens of Montgomery knew they were in for a long struggle.

The bus boycott lasted for more than a year. It was a difficult time for Martin and Coretta, and sometimes they were frightened. Many people were angry about the boycott, and one day someone even threw a bomb at the King's house.

Although no one was hurt, the experience scared the family. Martin and Coretta still refused to back down.

In 1956, a Supreme Court order finally put a stop to the unfair rules of the Montgomery Bus Company. By that time, requests for Martin to help organize other nonviolent protests were pouring in from all across the nation. The boycott had shown what African Americans could do if they united to fight for their rights without resorting to violence.

AP Wide World Photos

MONTGOMERY CITIZENS, MOSTLY AFRICAN AMERICAN, GATHERED AT DIFFERENT TIMES DURING THE BUS BOYCOTT TO DISCUSS THE PROTEST AS A COMMUNITY.

AP Wide World Photos

WHEN THE SUPREME COURT DECIDED THE MONTGOMERY BUS COMPANY'S RULES WERE UNCONSTITUTIONAL, HUNDREDS GATHERED TO CELEBRATE.

UPI/Corbis/Bettmann

AFTER POLICE ARRESTED MARTIN DURING A PEACEFUL PROTEST, CORETTA ANSWERED QUESTIONS FOR REPORTERS. WHEN SHE ATTEMPTED TO VISIT HIM IN JAIL, THE POLICE SENT HER AWAY.

A Dangerous Path

As the *civil rights movement* grew, Martin resigned from his position at the church. The Kings moved to Atlanta so Martin could lead the Southern Christian Leadership Conference (SCLC), an organization created to pass his message across the South.

Martin had been offered many jobs with high salaries, but he had turned them down. He took no money from the SCLC. The King family lived on a small income from Ebenezer Baptist Church, where his father was the pastor and Martin was co-pastor.

People frequently asked Martin to speak at events around the country and to help organize peaceful protests. As Martin's responsibilities grew, so did the demands on Coretta. She now had four small children: Yolanda, Martin Luther King III, Dexter, and Bernice. Not only was she busy at home, but she also traveled with Martin.

THE KING FAMILY AT THE DINNER TABLE. AS MARTIN'S FAME GREW, HE TRAVELED MORE FREQUENTLY. THE KINGS CHERISHED THEIR FAMILY TIME TOGETHER.

© Flip Schulke/Black Star

In addition, Coretta had found a way to use her musical talent. She gave a performance at New York's Town Hall, using poetry, dramatic readings, protest songs, and *spirituals* to tell the story of the civil rights movement. The audience found the combination of words and song effective and inspiring. Coretta soon received requests from all over the country for more "Freedom Concerts."

Coretta shared her husband's belief that the problems Black Americans experienced could be solved without violence. She also believed the civil rights movement was part of a larger goal: world peace. In 1962, she was named a *delegate* to the Women's Strike for Peace in Geneva, Switzerland. She joined women from all over the world who hoped to urge the Russian and American governments to stop testing nuclear weapons.

Even though Coretta was traveling a great deal, the needs of her family always came first. More and more, Martin's work took him away from home. Coretta fully understood the danger her husband faced each day. Whenever they said good-bye, she knew she might not see him again.

Many southerners adamantly opposed the idea that Black Americans deserved civil rights, and Martin's efforts angered them. Sometimes they attacked him; other times the police arrested him during protests. Coretta feared for Martin's safety, but she truly believed they were doing the right thing.

UPI/Corbis-Bettmann

POLICE ARREST MARTIN AT A PROTEST.

AP Wide World

CORETTA DEDICATED AS MUCH TIME AS SHE COULD TO
THE CIVIL RIGHTS MOVEMENT, BUT FAMILY WAS ALWAYS
HER FIRST CONCERN.

AP Wide World

THOUSANDS OF PEOPLE FROM ALL OVER THE COUNTRY GATHERED IN ATLANTA TO HONOR MARTIN LUTHER KING, JR., AND JOIN THE FUNERAL PROCESSION.

On April 4, 1968, Martin Luther King, Jr., was *assassinated*. Coretta had suffered a lot by this time, and she remained strong. The next day, she made a statement to the press. Coretta told the people that both she and Martin had known his life might be cut short. They both felt it wasn't how long one lived that was important, but how well one lived.

Coretta urged those who had admired her husband to help carry on his work. The day before his funeral, she took Martin's place in a civil rights march he was to have led in Memphis, Tennessee. Thousands of people came to join her from across the country. Thousands more stood along the route in silent tribute to the memory of a courageous leader and the bravery of his widow.

CORETTA AND THE KING CHILDREN AT MARTIN'S FUNERAL.

In Martin's Memory

After Martin died, Coretta committed herself even more firmly to the goals she had shared with her husband. She realized how important it was that she continue to do not only her own work, but Martin's as well. She went in his place to events he had planned to attend. At a peace rally in New York, she spoke from his notes. Just months after his death, Coretta called upon American women to "unite and form a solid block of women power" to fight racism, poverty, and war.

That same year, she founded the Martin Luther King, Jr., Center for Nonviolent Social Change as a memorial to her husband. The King Center has continued to grow, and more than three million people visited it every year. Visitors learn about King's ideas and goals. Coretta was the president of the organization until 1994, when her son Dexter took over the position. She continues to dedicate much of her time to the King Center, which sponsors programs and events in the name of world peace, human rights, and freedom.

UPI/Corbis-Bettmann

THE DAY BEFORE MARTIN'S FUNERAL, CORETTA ATTENDED A CIVIL RIGHTS DEMONSTRATION THAT MARTIN WAS TO HAVE LED.

UPI/Corbis-Bettmann

CORETTA SPOKE TO MINORITY WOMEN AT A NATIONAL FEMINIST
CONFERENCE. THE ATTENDEES RESOLVED TO END DISCRIMINATION
BASED ON BOTH RACE AND GENDER.

UPI/Corbis-Bettmann

POLICE ARRESTED CORETTA AND TWO OF HER CHILDREN WHEN THEY
PROTESTED APARTHEID, THE SOUTH AFRICAN GOVERNMENT'S POLICY
OF SEGREGATION, WHICH WAS FINALLY ABOLISHED IN 1992.

Over the years, Coretta has served on many political committees, and various organizations have recognized her important contributions. President Jimmy Carter appointed her to several positions, including a one-year assignment to the United Nations. Since 1970, The Coretta Scott King Award, honoring her courage and determination, has been awarded to Black authors and illustrators of quality books.

In 1985, Coretta and two of her children, Bernice and Martin III, were arrested outside the South African Embassy in Washington, D.C. Just as Martin led protests against the mistreatment of African Americans, the King family was now protesting racism outside the United States: *apartheid*, the policy of strict segregation imposed on South African Blacks.

For years Coretta worked to make Martin's birthday a national holiday. In 1986, Congress finally approved the plan, and the first celebration of Martin Luther King Day, the first American holiday dedicated to a Black American, was held on the third Monday of January. In 1994, Coretta testified before the Senate, telling members of a special committee that Martin Luther King Day should be a day in which Americans dedicate their time to public service, not to recreation.

CORETTA AND VICE PRESIDENT GEORGE BUSH LOOK ON AS PRESIDENT RONALD REAGAN SIGNS A BILL TO MAKE MARTIN'S BIRTHDAY A NATIONAL HOLIDAY.

AP Wide World Photos

Coretta Scott King still spends much of her time traveling to speak to people around the country, proclaiming the right to freedom and respect for all people. Recognized as one of America's most influential Black leaders, Coretta, together with her children, continues the fight to bring a nonviolent end to racism and prejudice in the United States and around the world.

IN APRIL 1994, THE KING'S SON DEXTER PROUDLY TOOK OVER CORETTA'S LEADERSHIP OF THE KING CENTER.

Reuters/Jeff Slate/Archive Photos

IN JANUARY 1998, CORETTA INTRODUCED A NEW BOOK, *I HAVE A DREAM*, NAMED FOR HER HUSBAND'S FAMOUS SPEECH AT THE 1968 CIVIL RIGHTS MARCH IN WASHINGTON, D.C.

AP Wide World Photos

Timeline

1927	Coretta Scott is born in Heiberger, Alabama.
1929	The Great Depression begins.
1937	The Scotts move into their new home.
1942	The Scotts home is burned down.
1943	Edythe Scott, Coretta's sister, is the first African American to attend Antioch College in Ohio.
1945	Coretta enrolls at Antioch College.
1951	Coretta leaves Antioch for Boston, where she attends the New England Conservatory of Music.
1952	Coretta meets Martin Luther King, Jr.
1953	Coretta and Martin marry in Marion, Alabama.
1954	Martin accepts a job as the minister of the Dexter Avenue Baptist Church in Montgomery, Alabama.
1955	Rosa Parks is arrested for refusing to give up her seat to a White man. Martin and Coretta encourage their community to hold a bus boycott.
1956	The U.S. Supreme Court rules that segregated buses are unconstitutional.
1962	Coretta attends the Women's Strike for Peace in Geneva, Switzerland.
1968	Martin is assassinated. Coretta commits herself to continuing his work. She begins fund-raising efforts to establish the Martin Luther King, Jr., Center for Nonviolent Social Change.
1970	The first Coretta Scott King Book Award is presented.
1981	The Martin Luther King, Jr., Center for Nonviolent Social Change opens in Atlanta, Georgia. Coretta is president of the center.
1985	Coretta and her children, Bernice and Martin III, are arrested during a protest against apartheid.
1986	Martin's birthday becomes a national holiday.
1994	Coretta's son, Dexter, becomes the new president of the Martin Luther King, Jr., Center for Nonviolent Social Change.

Glossary

African Americans
Americans whose ancestors came from the African continent. In the past, African Americans have been called colored people and Negroes.

apartheid
The former policy of the South African government of segregating Whites and non-Whites. Apartheid was abolished in 1992 when White voters approved a proposal to end it.

assassinate
To murder a prominent individual, usually a leader in politics or government.

boycott
To refuse to have dealings with a person or organization as a means to show disapproval of certain conditions.

civil rights
The rights guaranteed to all American citizens by the Constitution and its amendments.

civil rights movement
The protests and political action of African American and White activists who worked to achieve civil rights and equality for minorities during the 1950s and 1960s.

delegate
A person who is named as a representative to an important event.

Great Depression
A period beginning in 1929 during which there was little economic activity in the United States, and unemployment rose to high levels.

prejudice
A bad feeling or opinion about something or someone without just reason; feeling anger toward a group or its characteristics.

racism
The belief that one race is naturally superior, or better, than another.

scholarship
An award of money given to a successful student to be used toward his or her education.

segregated
To be separated or isolated because of race, class, or ethnic group.

spirituals
Religious songs written by African American slaves in the southern United States.

Index

For Further Reading

Henry, Sondra, and Taitz, Emily. *Coretta Scott King: Keeper of the Dream.* Springfield, NJ: Enslow Publishers, 1992.

King, Coretta Scott. *My Life With Martin Luther King, Jr.* New York, NY: Henry Holt, 1994.

Weber, Michael. *The African American Civil Rights Movement (Causes and Consequences).* Austin, TX: Raintree/Steck Vaughn, 1998.

Web sites
The following sites contain information about Martin Luther King, Jr., and the Center for non-violent change:
http://www-leland.stanford.edu/group/King
http://www.nps.gov/malu/index.html
http://www.thekingcenter.com

For general information about African Americans and other resources to study:
http://www.msstate.edu/Archives/History/USA/Afro-Amer/afro.html

To contact the King Center:
The King Center
449 Auburn Avenue, NE
Atlanta, GA 30312
Tel. 404-524-1956